HAL•LEONARD
INSTRUMENTAL PLAY-ALONG

CELLO

T0083347

AUDIO ACCESS INCLUDED

PLAYBACK+
Speed • Pitch • Balance • Loop

HIT SONGS

Audio arrangements by Peter Deneff

To access audio, visit:
www.halleonard.com/mylibrary

Enter Code
2775-0255-7870-7986

ISBN 978-1-70515-017-7

HAL•LEONARD®

Visit Hal Leonard Online at
www.halleonard.com

Contact us:
Hal Leonard
7777 West Bluemound Road
Milwaukee, WI 53213
Email: info@halleonard.com

In Europe, contact:
Hal Leonard Europe Limited
42 Wigmore Street
Marylebone, London, W1U 2RN
Email: info@halleonardeurope.com

In Australia, contact:
Hal Leonard Australia Pty. Ltd.
4 Lentara Court
Cheltenham, Victoria, 3192 Australia
Email: info@halleonard.com.au

CONTENTS

4   Adore You

5   Anyone

6   Bad Habits

7   Bang!

8   Blinding Lights

10   Circles

12   Drivers License

14   Heather

16   Kings & Queens

18   Señorita

15   Therefore I Am

20   Willow

22   Without You

ADORE YOU

Cello

Words and Music by HARRY STYLES,
THOMAS HULL, TYLER JOHNSON
and AMY ALLEN

ANYONE

CELLO

Words and Music by JUSTIN BIEBER,
JON BELLION, JORDAN JOHNSON,
ALEXANDER IZQUIERDO, ANDREW WATT,
RAUL CUBINA, STEFAN JOHNSON
and MICHAEL POLLACK

BAD HABITS

CELLO

Words and Music by ED SHEERAN,
JOHNNY McDAID and FRED GIBSON

BANG!

CELLO

Words and Music by ADAM METZGER,
JACK METZGER and RYAN METZGER

BLINDING LIGHTS

CELLO

Words and Music by ABEL TESFAYE,
MAX MARTIN, JASON QUENNEVILLE,
OSCAR HOLTER and AHMAD BALSHE

CIRCLES

Cello

Words and Music by AUSTIN POST,
KAAN GUNESBERK, LOUIS BELL,
WILLIAM WALSH and ADAM FEENEY

DRIVERS LICENSE

CELLO

Words and Music by OLIVIA RODRIGO
and DANIEL NIGRO

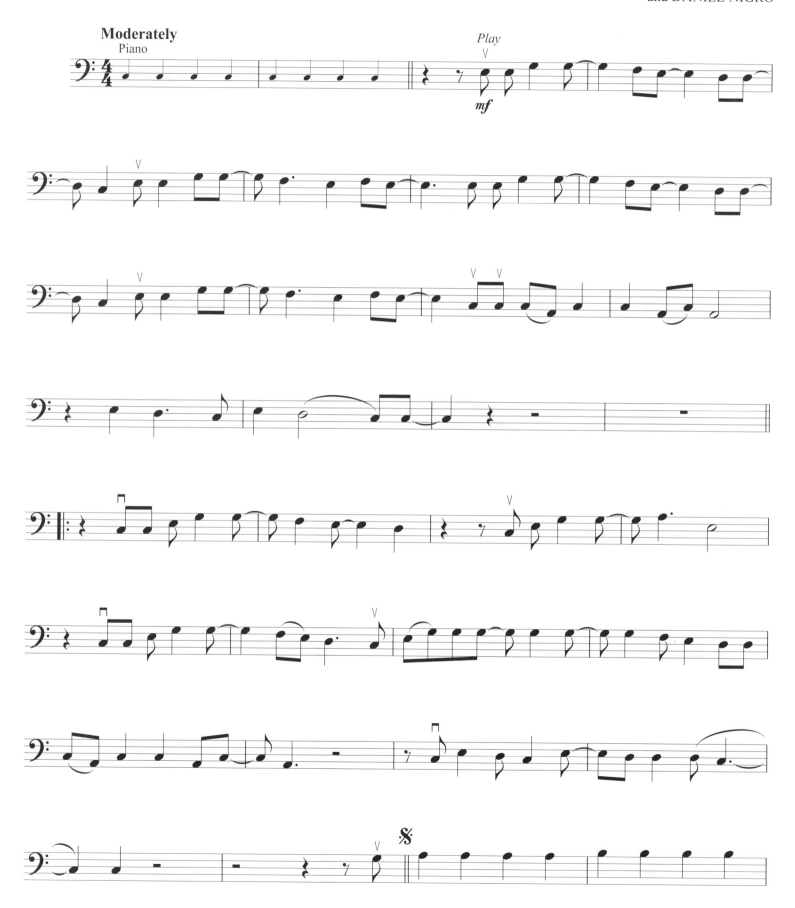

HEATHER

CELLO

Words and Music by
CONAN GRAY

THEREFORE I AM

CELLO

Words and Music by BILLIE EILISH O'CONNELL
and FINNEAS O'CONNELL

KINGS & QUEENS

CELLO

Words and Music by DESMOND CHILD,
AMANDA KOCI, BRETT McLAUGHLIN,
HENRY WALTER, MADISON LOVE,
HILLARY BERNSTEIN, JAKOB ERIXSON,
MIMOZA BLINSON and NADIR KHAYAT

D.S. al Coda

CODA

SEÑORITA

CELLO

Words and Music by CAMILA CABELLO,
CHARLOTTE AITCHISON, JACK PATTERSON,
SHAWN MENDES, MAGNUS HØIBERG,
BENJAMIN LEVIN, ALI TAMPOSI
and ANDREW WOTMAN

Moderately

WILLOW

CELLO

Words and Music by TAYLOR SWIFT
and AARON DESSNER

WITHOUT YOU

CELLO

Words and Music by BLAKE SLATKIN,
OMER FEDI, BILLY WALSH
and CHARLTON HOWARD